France

Tom Streissguth

✺ Carolrhoda Books, Inc. / Minneapolis

Photo Acknowledgments

Photographs, maps, and artworks are used courtesy of: John Erste, pp. 1, 2–3, 27, 35, 40–41; Laura Westlund, pp. 4–5, 19, 28–29, 33, 38–39, 43, 45; © Robert Fried, pp. 6, 9 (right and bottom), 11, 12, 13 (left), 14, 15 (top and bottom), 17 (left and right), 18, 20 (top), 21, 22 (bottom), 23, 26 (top), 28, 30, 31 (left), 32, 33, 35, 37 (bottom); Buddy Mays/TRAVEL STOCK, pp. 7, 13 (right), 20 (bottom), 24, 27, 37 (top); © Michele Burgess, pp. 8, 10; French Government Tourist Office, pp. 9 (left), 25 (top right by Fred Slavin), 42 (bottom); © Eugene G. Schulz, pp. 13 (middle), 42 (top); © M. Kimak, pp. 16, 29; Chris Fairclough, pp. 22 (top), 31 (right), 36; Bob Wolfe, p. 25 (left); American Egg Board, p. 25 (bottom right); Burch Communications, Inc., p. 26 (bottom); A. A. M. van der Heyden, p. 34; Sportschrome, p. 38; Parc Astérix, p. 41; Erich Lessing/Art Resource, NY, p. 43; Independent Picture Service, p. 44. Cover photo of a grape harvester © Robert Fried.

Carolrhoda Books, Inc.
c/o The Lerner Publishing Group
241 First Avenue North
Minneapolis, Minnesota 55401 U.S.A.
Website address: www.lernerbooks.com

Recipe for Poires Hélène adapted from *Cooking the French Way* by Lynne Marie Waldee (Minneapolis: Lerner Publications Company, 1982).

Words in **bold type** are explained in a glossary that begins on page 44.

Library of Congress Cataloging-in-Publication Data

Streissguth, Thomas, 1958–
     France / by Tom Streissguth.
          p.   cm. — (Globe-trotters club)
     Includes index.
     Summary: An overview of France, emphasizing its cultural aspects.
     ISBN 1–57505–103–6 (alk. paper)
     1. France—Juvenile literature. [1. France.] I. Title. II. Series:
  Globe-trotters club (series)
DC29.3.S75   1997
944—dc 20   96–38732

Manufactured in the United States of America
1 2 3 4 5 6 – JR – 02 01 00 99 98 97

Contents

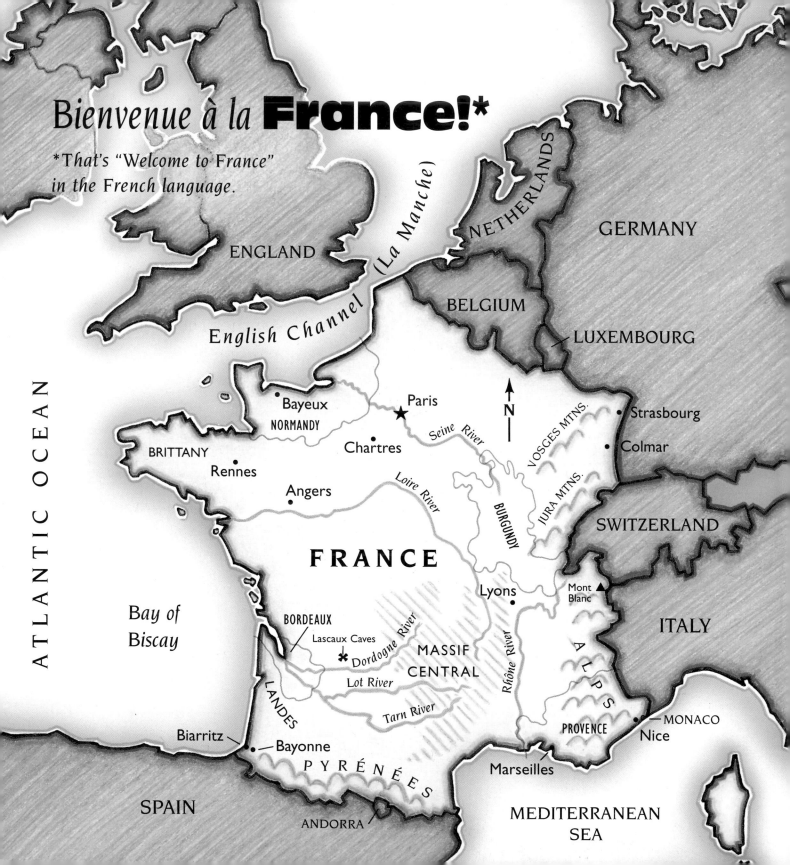

Bienvenue à la **France!***

*That's "Welcome to France" in the French language.

ENGLAND

English Channel (La Manche)

NETHERLANDS

GERMANY

BELGIUM

LUXEMBOURG

ATLANTIC OCEAN

N

• Bayeux
NORMANDY
★ Paris

Strasbourg

Seine River

VOSGES MTNS.

Colmar

BRITTANY
• Rennes
Chartres

Loire River

JURA MTNS.

• Angers

BURGUNDY

SWITZERLAND

FRANCE

Bay of Biscay

Lyons

Mont Blanc ▲

ITALY

BORDEAUX
Lascaux Caves
✶
Dordogne River

MASSIF CENTRAL

A L P S

Lot River

Rhône River

LANDES

Tarn River

PROVENCE

MONACO
Nice

Biarritz
• Bayonne

P Y R É N É E S

Marseilles

SPAIN

ANDORRA

MEDITERRANEAN SEA

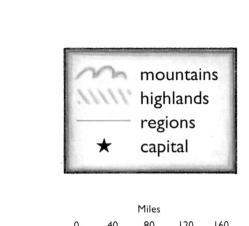

mountains	
highlands	
regions	
★ capital	

Miles

0 40 80 120 160

0 80 160 240

Kilometers

Take a look at this map of France. You'll notice that of the country's six sides, three touch water and three touch land. Off the northwest coast a famous **strait** (a narrow waterway that connects two larger bodies of water) separates France from England. The French call this body of water La Manche. The English call it the English Channel.

On the western side of France lies the Bay of Biscay, an arm of the Atlantic Ocean. The Atlantic often brings rainy weather to this part of the country. The ocean's winds also keep temperatures near the western coast from getting too hot in summer or too cold in winter.

France's southeastern coast faces the Mediterranean Sea. Provence, the name for this corner of France, is warm and dry. The Alps, a towering mountain range, shelter the coast from cold winds and rain. Mont Blanc, the tallest Alp, is the highest point in all of western Europe.

Q. What has six sides and is filled with good food?

A. The country of France, or La République Française, as the nation is known in French.

5

(Left) **In southwestern France, a farmhouse nestles among the Pyrénées.** (Facing page) **A farmer in southern France walks between neat rows of grapevines.**

Three Touch **Land**

 A tall mountain range called the Pyrénées lies in the southwest of France. On the other side of these mountains is the country of Spain. The Roman Empire conquered France and Spain 2,000 years ago. The Roman's culture and language spread throughout the empire.

Italy, Switzerland, and Germany lie east of France. In the last 100 years or so, France and Germany have fought several times over lands in eastern France. Some people living in the area speak German, and many of the towns along the French-German border have German names.

Plains stretch along the northeast, where France meets Belgium and Luxembourg. Farmers plant crops of wheat and sugar beets in this broad, flat area.

France covers a lot of western Europe. In fact, except for Russia, France is the biggest country in Europe.

The Massif Central

Much of the land in France is rolling hills. A **plateau** (an area of high, level land) called the Massif Central dominates southern France. Massif Central means "central highlands." Here many round black-stone mounds rise steeply from the ground. Volcanoes formed these mounds a long time ago.

Several rivers start in the Massif Central. These waterways include the Dordogne, the Lot, the Tarn, and the Loire, which is the country's longest river. Two other important rivers in France are the Seine, which goes through the capital city of Paris, and the Rhône. The Rhône begins in Switzerland, flows south through France, and lets out at the Mediterranean Sea. Vineyards are located not far from where the Rhône River reaches the sea.

Paris—Where **It's At**

Paris is France's capital and largest city. In fact, Paris is the center of just about everything—government, business, and the arts. Some French think Paris is noisy and too crowded to live in. But they sure like to visit!

Paris was once just a village on a small island in the Seine River. As the village grew, a big church called Notre Dame de Paris was built. The French writer Victor Hugo wrote a book about this cathedral called *The Hunchback of Notre Dame*. You may have heard of it. The hero was a bell ringer named Quasimodo.

The village needed more land and spread out from the island onto both banks (sides) of the Seine River. The north side of the Seine is called the Right Bank. The south side is the Left Bank.

From high up in the Eiffel Tower, you can see how big Paris really is!

In and around Paris

The Eiffel Tower— This landmark, built in 1889 for the world's fair, proved that cast iron was strong enough to support tall structures. From the top, you'll get a better view of Paris than most birds.

The Arc de Triomphe— A French emperor named Napoléon had the arch built to celebrate his army's many victories. An airplane once flew through the arch. No kidding!

Versailles—The French kings lived in this royal palace. A treaty signed here in the late 1700s ended the American Revolution between Britain and the United States.

Side Swipe In France, traffic circles have taken the place of many intersections. Drivers go around as far as they need to and then exit in the desired direction.

Traveling the
Hexagon

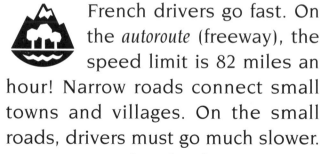 French drivers go fast. On the *autoroute* (freeway), the speed limit is 82 miles an hour! Narrow roads connect small towns and villages. On the small roads, drivers must go much slower.

Many people who live in cities don't bother owning a car. If they want to go somewhere, they hop on a train. One kind of passenger train used in France is the *train à grande vitesse*, or TGV. That means high-speed train. A TGV cruises at about 186 miles an hour. On test runs, TGVs have zipped along at 320 miles in one hour! High-speed trains travel between Paris, Lyons, Bordeaux, and other big cities.

In the 1600s, French engineers built a network of canals to link France's major rivers. These canals made it possible to sail across France, from the English Channel to the Mediterranean Sea, instead of all the way around Spain. Commercial boats don't use them anymore, but houseboats and small barges float along the canals, just for fun.

(Left) **Canals offer a relaxing way to travel through France. (Above) Cars cruise along France's miles and miles of freeway. This freeway runs between the cities of Strasbourg and Colmar in northeastern France.**

Fast Facts about France

Name: La République Française
(Republic of France)

Area: 212,935 square miles

Main Landforms: Alps, Brittany Peninsula, Jura Mountains, Massif Central, Pyrénées, Vosges Mountains

Highest Point: Mont Blanc (15,771 feet)

Lowest Point: Below sea level

Animals: Boar, hares, quail, fox, deer, grouse, red squirrels, nightingales

Capital City: Paris

Other Major Cities: Marseilles, Lyons, Toulouse, Nice, Bordeaux

Official Language: French

Monetary Unit: Franc

Bonjour! French teenagers wave hello from a park near Paris.

The French **People**

The ancestors of the **ethnic French** came from groups of long-ago settlers and invaders. Gauls, Romans, Franks, Normans, and Basques arrived from different areas of Europe, At some point, each ruled parts of France. This helps explain why ethnic French don't always look alike or speak the same second language.

The Gauls, the earliest residents of France, got pushed aside by the Romans. The Gauls ended up in Brittany, the long arm of France that juts westward into the Atlantic Ocean. In Brittany you might hear Breton—a Celtic language that is related to the ancient languages of Ireland, Scotland, and Wales.

The Basques still live in the southwestern corner of France. And many Basques speak Euskara, their traditional language, as well as French.

In the south, where most Romans settled, many French people have darker skin and hair. They may have ancestors from Mediterranean countries such as Italy or Spain.

Some northern French have blond hair and blue eyes. Those features may come from the Normans who sailed southward from the Scandinavian countries of Norway, Sweden, and Denmark.

A fruit vendor (below) **in the city of Lyons and sunbathers** (right) **along the coast of La Manche (the English Channel)**

A woman from the Provence region heads home from the market.

Newcomers from **All Over**

 At one time, France owned many territories, or **colonies,** on the continents of Asia and Africa. France still has some of these overseas lands, including islands in the Caribbean Sea and in the South Pacific Ocean.

France lost many of its colonies after World War II, which ended in 1945. But the French government gave the people who lived in the colonies the right to immigrate (move) to France. **Immigrants** came from the countries of Algeria, Morocco, and Vietnam. Most of them stayed in big cites.

The largest group of immigrants in France is from **North Africa.** They have settled in southern France or in the suburbs of Paris. Many of these immigrants work in low-paying jobs that most French workers don't want.

These days, France has lots of jobless ethnic French, who believe the immigrants are taking away jobs. These French want the government to stop immigrants from coming to France. But the immigrants know they have a right to settle in France. They want to stay in France, where they can make a better life for their families.

(Facing page) **Modern France is home to ethnic French as well as to people with North African backgrounds.** (Top) **Immigrants from Tunisia, North Africa, run this** *patisserie* **(bakery).** (Right) **An ethnic Moroccan woman who works for the French national railway supplies travel information to train passengers.**

Bumper to bumper, cars crowd the road in Paris.

City and Country **Living**

 Compared to the rest of Europe, much of France isn't very crowded. Young people, when they're old enough, often move to the cities. Many choose Paris as their home. New suburbs sprout up farther and farther away from the city. Paris and the towns nearby make up the largest **metropolitan area** in Europe.

French cities are busy places. Traffic whizzes by on the streets, and pedestrians jostle one another on the narrow sidewalks. People get to their jobs by nine o'clock. When the long lunch break begins at noon, the streets suddenly become quiet. Stores and offices close. At two o'clock, everything starts up again and stays open in the evening until six or seven o'clock.

When asked to imagine the best place to live, city dwellers often answer: a small farm. In the country-side, life moves more slowly. Small

Villagers enjoy a walk in the local park.

Farm chores are part of life in the Basque region.

villages often have only one store, one restaurant, one factory, and one main road. People gather in the park at the center of town, where they play and exchange news. Thousands of small family farms dot the coun-tryside. Farm kids help milk the cows and feed the chickens before school.

17

Parlez-Vous **Français?**

That's French for "Do you speak French?" If you do, you know there are many differences between French and English. For example, French people must choose how to address one

Franglais

Many English words have crept into French people's daily speech. The French word for English is *anglais*. So some people call this new French-English vocabulary *franglais*.

Here are some franglais words—le hamburger, le weekend, and le fast food. Can you figure out what they mean? Many French people don't like franglais. To them, it seems as if the English language is taking over.

Oh, no, franglais! La Sandwicherie serves hot and cold sandwiches. Many French won't use English words, such as sandwich, that have begun to appear in the French language.

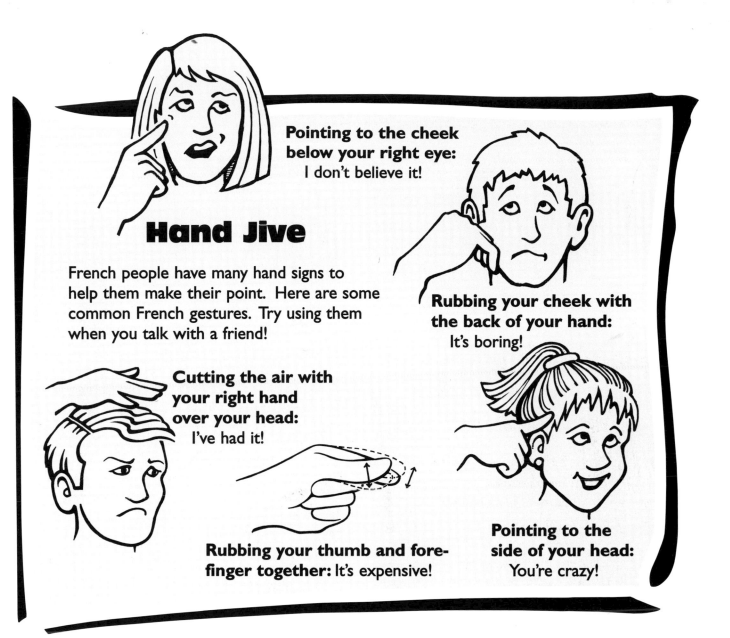

Hand Jive

French people have many hand signs to help them make their point. Here are some common French gestures. Try using them when you talk with a friend!

Pointing to the cheek below your right eye: I don't believe it!

Rubbing your cheek with the back of your hand: It's boring!

Cutting the air with your right hand over your head: I've had it!

Rubbing your thumb and forefinger together: It's expensive!

Pointing to the side of your head: You're crazy!

another. Grownups can use *tu* to mean "you" when speaking to a friend, a relative, a child, or a pet. But they can't use tu when speaking to a stranger and especially not to the boss! To be polite, adults choose the *vous* form of address. Vous also means "you." Children always use vous when speaking to adults—except for their parents.

City folks in France tend to live in apartments. These are in Biarritz, a resort along the Bay of Biscay.

Homes line the roads in some French villages.

Home Sweet
Home

What's a French home like? In the cities, most people live in apartments that were built long ago. The doorway to the apartment house stands just a few feet from the busy street. Inside, a dark staircase usually winds to the upper floors. In many old buildings, a wall switch in the lobby turns on a light so you can see. But don't waste time! The light will go off automatically after 30 seconds. Some of these apartments are very small—only a bedroom and one or two other rooms.

On the edges of cities and in the nearby towns, apartments are larger. Families may have a living room, dining room, a small kitchen, and two or three bedrooms. French apartments split the bathroom into two parts. One room is for washing up or taking a shower, and another room—the size of a narrow closet—houses the toilet.

In towns and villages, rows of houses sometimes face the park, or village green. Ivy vines cover many of the old stone houses. Below the shuttered windows, geraniums bloom in planters. Flower beds and vegetable gardens fill many of the yards. Farmhouses in the country tend to be bigger.

Castles on the Loire

The winding Loire River Valley is the setting for many of France's castles. Centuries ago, kings, queens, and other nobility lived here.

Some castles—built as long ago as the ninth century—served as fortresses to protect the area from invaders. Through narrow slits, soldiers defended the estates with arrows, crossbows, and spears. If prisoners were caught, they could be housed in the castles' dungeons.

The château (castle) at Angers dates to the 1200s.

Family *Life*

French families used to be very large. In some households, children grew up with aunts, uncles, and grandparents all living under the same roof.

But modern French families—especially in the cities—are smaller. Most parents have only one or two

(Above) **A boy gets advice from his dad on bike repair.** (Below) **Family members wait to dig into fondue. To eat this dish, each diner skewers small pieces of meat and cooks them at the table in a common pot.**

All in the Family

Here are the French words for family members. Practice these terms on your own family. See if they can understand you!

father	*père*	(PEHR)
mother	*mère*	(MEHR)
uncle	*oncle*	(OH[n]-kluh)
aunt	*tante*	(TAH[n]T)
grandfather	*grand-père*	(grah[n]-PEHR)
grandmother	*grand-mère*	(grah[n]-MEHR)
son	*fils*	(FEES)
daughter	*fille*	(FEE)
brother	*frère*	(FREHR)
sister	*sœur*	(SUR)

children. Relatives may also live farther away from one another. When children finish school, they may move far from home.

Many families get together every Sunday. When relatives come to visit, everyone greets everyone else with a handshake and a *bisou*. This is a little kiss on each cheek—first the right, then the left. Then they sit down at the table for hours, enjoying good food and conversation.

Bon **Appétit!**

Bon appétit! French people want you to enjoy your meal and so wish you "good appetite!" And all over the world people love to cook and eat foods that the French made first. In fact, many food words in the English language come from France, including casserole, quiche, **crêpe,** and **vinaigrette.**

Fancy French cooking can be tricky. Many restaurants serve food that's topped with tasty sauces. Most meals at home are simpler. Dinner may take place in stages called courses. The meal starts with appetizers—a plate of ham, pickles, pâté (chopped meat flavored with spices), or hard-boiled eggs with mayonnaise. The main course includes meat or fish, with vegetables. Almost every meal involves long, thin, crunchy loaves of bread called

Parisians get up early to buy the freshest baguettes.

baguettes. Next comes a green salad, and then a plate of cheeses. Oftentimes, the meal ends with fruit. On special occasions, the French enjoy an elegant cake or pastry.

Poires Hélène

The French name sounds fancier than the English name—Pears Helen. But whichever language you use, you and three other people will love eating this dessert.

½ cup chocolate syrup
4 to 8 scoops vanilla ice cream
4 canned pear halves, drained
⅓ cup raspberry or strawberry jam
1 tablespoon hot water

1. In 4 dessert glasses or bowls, pour 2 tablespoons chocolate syrup.
2. Place 1 to 2 scoops of ice cream on top of the syrup.
3. Put 1 pear half, flat-side down, on the ice cream.
4. Mix jam and water in a separate bowl. Spoon over each pear.

Cheese (above) **and quiche** (below) **are French favorites.**

25

Regional **Foods**

Each region in France prepares its own special food. The people of Burgundy, in eastern France, like to eat escargots (snails). Bretons (people from Brittany) often eat thin pancakes called crêpes. Normandy's apples go into

(Right) **Along the Mediterranean Sea, crews haul in fish for a stew called bouillabaisse.** (Below) **Crêpes stuffed with ham and broccoli make a mouth-watering meal.**

The Big Cheese

French shoppers can pick from several hundred different kinds of cheeses. In France, some say there's a different cheese for each day of the year.

The most popular cheese is Camembert, which comes from Normandy. The cheese comes in a round box and gets softer—and smellier—as it gets older. A date stamped on the side of the box lets you know when you'll want to eat the cheese. If you like firm cheese, you have to eat it one month before the date. If you like semi-firm cheese, then you eat Camembert two weeks before. If you like your cheese soft and strong flavored, then you wait a bit more than a week before the date to eat the cheese.

Le Pew

cider and pastries. On the Mediterranean coast, a fish stew called bouillabaisse uses seafood caught nearby.

The French are known for their fine foods. Have you ever eaten snails, tripe, liver, frog legs, sheep's brains, or eel? You might if you visited France! Wild mushrooms called truffles are another special treat. Hunters use pigs to sniff out the rare mushrooms in the woods.

Food and **Treasures**

In France shoppers can buy food in *hypermarchés*. You can find almost anything at these huge supermarkets, and they are open all day. But many people prefer to shop in smaller stores that specialize in just one kind of food, like bread, meat, or cheese. These small shops open in the morning and close in the early afternoon.

On certain days, shoppers can buy food at an outdoor market. Stalls line the sidewalks. Vendors sell vegetables, fruits, meat, flowers, and much more. Vegetable sellers sing about tomatoes and artichokes. Laughter and arguments from the fish stall fill the air. Shoppers with straw baskets wander slowly. People may bring along their small dogs for the fun. *Waouf! Waouf!*

This market in Bayonne, southwestern France, is filled floor to ceiling with pineapples, artichokes, and many other types of fruits and vegetables.

oeufs, fromages—butter, eggs, and cheese.

Sharp-eyed shoppers look for a good deal on jeans at a Parisian flea market.

Some towns also have a *marché aux puces*, or "flea market." Sellers spread secondhand goods on tables or on the ground. Shoppers look for treasures. Paris has the world's biggest flea market—it's called Les Puces de St. Ouen.

But Paris is also the fashion capital of the world. Each year designers create new styles of clothing. All eyes are on Paris when models show the creations at fashion shows.

WAOUF!

Did you know that one out of three households in France has a pet dog? The French word for dog is *chien*. French dogs say *waouf, waouf.*

(Left) **With help from her teacher, a French student struggles through a tough math problem.** (Facing Page) **French students of all ages play soccer—called** *football* **in French—after school and in the summer.**

Kid Seasons—
School and Summer

Do you want to visit a French school? Classes begin at eight or nine o'clock in the morning and continue until four or five o'clock in the afternoon. On Wednesdays, schools are closed. French kids go to classes on Saturday mornings instead. The school year runs from early September until the end of June. That may seem long, but students get lots of breaks for holidays.

French kids study science, civics, history, geography, math, French, and foreign languages. Every night they read and do homework. Teachers fill out report cards three times a year.

French kids don't goof off in the summer either. Every town or village has a summer camp in a park or nearby forest. The French call these camps *centre aire*, or "fresh air centers." During the work week, parents drive their kids to the camps. Counselors keep a close eye on the campers, who use the playgrounds and soccer fields and the indoor areas for games and crafts. After work, parents pick up their kids.

A Boy from Brittany

Meet 11-year-old Pascal Gué. He's from Rennes, an old city in the northwestern region of France called Brittany. Pascal goes to an elementary school near his high-rise apartment building. Next year he'll enter a *lycée* (secondary school). But before that he needs to brush up on his math and grammar skills!

Faiths of **France**

France doesn't have an official religion. But three out of four people in France belong to the Roman Catholic Church. Smaller numbers of the French are Islamic, Protestant, or Jewish.

A stone or brick Catholic church stands near the center of every French city and town. But in important cities, the French built magnificent churches called cathedrals. Workers began building many of the cathedrals about nine centuries ago. Construction sometimes took as long as two hundred years. Cathedrals can be hundreds of feet tall. Stained-glass windows rise along the high side walls. The pictures in the windows illustrate Bible stories because in those days many people did not read.

In France about one out of every seven people goes to church regularly. People do get married and baptized in their local church, but many small churches don't even offer daily or weekly services. Noël (Christmas) and Pâques (Easter) are the most important Christian holidays in France. On these holidays, people crowd into the churches to celebrate.

A Roman Catholic priest blesses a young couple when they get married.

Gothic Supports

The designers of French cathedrals invented a building style that has come to be called Gothic architecture. **Flying buttresses**—a type of arched support set against the outside walls—took on much of the roof's weight. Since the walls no longer had to do all the work of holding up the roof, they could be filled with huge stained-glass windows.

This stained-glass window is part of the cathedral at Chartres.

Bastille Day celebrations include parades, fireworks, and music. Here, mounted soldiers surround the late president of France François Mitterrand (in blue suit) as his jeep makes its way down a Parisian street.

A *la* **Fête!**

It's July 14—Bastille Day! Crowds of people stand along a wide avenue in the center of Paris. Tanks and military cars parade by. A band plays the French national anthem, "La Marseillaise." Jets scream overhead

trailing blue, white, and red smoke. These are the three colors of the French flag.

Cities and towns throughout France celebrate Bastille Day, the French national holiday. On this day, the nation remembers a famous riot that took place in 1789. In an outburst of disorder, the people of Paris attacked the Bastille—a terrible prison. They began the French Revolution. Before the Revolution, the king of France had total power. The people of France fought this war because they wanted to have a say in how the country was run. On Bastille Day, fireworks burst over the streets. The country's flag waves above town halls.

Local festivals give the French a chance to enjoy themselves year-round. Proud of their fine wines, many towns host wine festivals in the fall. Drama, music, and folklore festivals entertain summer vacationers. The city of Nice hosts the Battle of Flowers in February.

Les Pennons de Lyon, a regional pageant held in the city of Lyons, dates to the 1200s. Participants wear costumes from the period and wave large colorful flags.

April Fish Day

On April 1, the French celebrate *Poisson d'avril,* or "April Fish." This holiday goes back to the 1500s, when the French king made January 1 the new New Year's Day. (The old New Year's Day had been April 1.) Some people didn't want to change the date of the holiday. They kept celebrating New Year's Day in April. Somehow these people got the name "April fish."

So now on April 1, French people cut a fish out of paper or cloth. They try to sneak up and stick the fish on a friend's back. Then others point to the victim and shout "Poisson d'avril!"

Vacation **Time**

Guess how many weeks of vacation French workers can take each year? Five weeks! All the vacation may be taken during the summer, but some families are beginning to take a shorter vacation in the summer so they can take a ski trip in the winter, too. In the cities, a lot of businesses close down during August because almost everyone leaves town.

Many families head to the beaches. Families may travel to the sunny Mediterranean coast. Another favorite spot is the Landes, an area on the Atlantic coast in southwestern France. Swimmers dive into the waves, and children tumble down the sand dunes. Some southern towns put on festivals with music, theater, and folk dancing.

The French love to camp and hike in the mountains. Other people meet relatives at their second home in the country. Kids swim and fish in the nearby rivers. They play *pétanque*, France's national game, with the adults.

Fishing is a fun summer pastime for French vacationers. What activities does your family enjoy on vacation?

to see who can get closest to the wooden target ball.

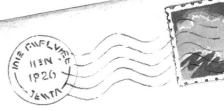

Dear Mom and Dad,
Today we went to a museum in a little town called Bayeux. The Bayeux Tapestry took a long time to look at—it is almost the length of a football field (I'm serious!) and only about two feet high. The scenes stitched on linen tell the story of how William the Conqueror from Normandy (part of northern France) became the king of England almost a thousand years ago. The tapestry is just about that old, too! Tomorrow we're going to the beaches on the English Channel.

See you soon!

Sium Mainittia
Waum Kaillim
Thaluruhu, Sim
7301, Laurattum

(Above left) **In winter some families travel to the snowy Alps to ski or sled.** (Left) **Pétanque competitions take place year-round. The object is for one team to place its large metal balls closer to the small wooden ball than the other team does.**

37

Racing **Fever**

Hundreds of bikes whoosh by on narrow country lanes. Motor scooters dart after them. Dozens of cars and vans filled with bicycle mechanics follow the racers. People along the roadside clap and yell. What's all the fuss? The Tour de France!

Bicycle racing is a big sport in France. Every summer some of the best cyclists from all over the world compete in the Tour de France. This race lasts three weeks and takes a different route every year. Riders go over plains and mountains, traveling through dozens of towns. The Tour always ends in Paris.

Each day of the race is called a stage. At the end of each stage, the person in first place is awarded a yellow bicycling shirt. He struggles a little to pull it on over the shirt he's been wearing all day.

(Facing page) **Hundreds of cyclists participate in the annual Tour de France. The grueling route challenges the athletes' fitness and concentration.**

Home Tour

Find a map of your state and design a bicycle tour through it. The tour should last one week. Each day riders should go about 100 miles, and the day's ride should end in a town. See if you can design the race to go through different kinds of land—some days the ride may be hilly, some days it may be flat. To end the race, the cyclists should race down a main street in your state capital.

At the end of the race, the overall winner poses in the yellow shirt near the finish line. The French are proud of the Tour de France, even if the winner is not always French. The newer Tour de France Féminin (a race for women) has been held yearly since 1984.

Read On!

French people of all ages love to read. Beauty and the Beast, Babar, and the Little Prince are famous characters from French fables and children's picture books. French kids still love the fairy tales collected 300 years ago by Charles Perrault. There's a good chance that you know these stories, too. Perrault's book was *Tales of Mother Goose*, which included the stories of "Sleeping Beauty," "Little Red Riding Hood," "Cinderella," and "Puss in Boots."

As they get older, French kids read the books written by other famous French writers. Victor Hugo, for example, wrote *The Hunchback of Notre Dame*. Hugo also told the story of the French Revolution in a book called *Les Misérables*. *The Three Musketeers* by Alexandre Dumas is also a French book.

The French respect their country's writers. If a writer is famous enough, he or she is chosen to be a member of the French Academy—the French writers' Hall of Fame.

Astérix

Astérix is one of the most popular French comic-book characters. The Astérix stories take place in a small village in ancient Gaul. The stubborn, proud people of the village hold out against the invading Romans. Astérix's village remains the last to be conquered. A lively warrior, Astérix always outfoxes the Romans.

In the streets and in the marketplace, the Gauls argue constantly. The stories always end with the characters seated around a big table, where they feast on good food.

To French readers, the village and the characters all seem strangely familiar. Just change the clothing, and the houses, and you could be anywhere in modern France.

Astérix

Obélix

The *Mona Lisa* (above) **by Leonardo da Vinci is probably the most famous painting in the Louvre. Horses** (below) **are among the animals that prehistoric artists painted on the walls of the Lascaux Caves.**

Adventures in **Art**

One way to get really tired feet in France is to go to the Louvre. This huge palace was turned into an art museum. Can you imagine walking through eight miles of art! The Louvre holds more than a million paintings, sculptures, drawings, pieces of jewelry, and other objects.

People who visit the museum need a good map to find their way around—or even to find their way out. The museum's main entrance is a glass pyramid that is much newer than the rest of the museum.

Not all art in France is found in museums. One day in 1940, four French boys were searching for their dog not far from the town of Lascaux. One of the boys fell into a very deep hole. When he looked around, he saw pictures of bison, horses, and a huge bull on the walls.

Painting with Points

The French painter Georges Seurat dabbed dots of paint on canvas—many thousands of dots in different colors! He dabbed certain colors next to one another on purpose. From a distance, the colors blend, becoming the shapes in the picture. This type of painting came to be called pointillism, because Seurat used the point of the paintbrush for the task.

Dab your own dots. Use a different cotton-tipped stick for each color. Dip the stick in the paint, then touch the paper with the tip. Place different colors side by side to create new colors. Do the colors form shapes when you stand back far enough?

The boys had discovered the Lascaux Caves in southwestern France. The cave paintings are thousands of years old. The huge crowds of curious tourists that came to see the art caused the caves' environment to change. A large amount of algae and bacteria grew and began to damage the paintings. The caves were closed in 1963. But you can see an exact copy of the paintings at a place called Lascaux II. Painters copied the originals, using the same kind of paint as the ancient artists did.

Sewn together, the long panels of the Bayeux Tapestry make one very long piece of cloth. At 230 feet, it's nearly the length of a football field. No kidding! The hand-stitched cloth depicts events from eleventh-century French history.

Glossary

baguette: A long, thin loaf of bread, often called French bread.

colony: A territory ruled by a country that is located far away.

crêpe: A very thin pancake, usually rolled up with a filling.

ethnic French: A person whose ancestors are from one of several European groups that invaded and settled in France.

flying buttress: An arched support put between an outside wall and a column that stands away from the wall. A flying buttress strengthens a wall.

immigrant: A person who moves from the home country to another country.

metropolitan area: A central city and the towns (suburbs) that have grown up around it.

North Africa: A region of the African continent that includes Morocco, Algeria, Tunisia, Libya, and Egypt.

plain: A large area of flat land.

plateau: A large area of high, level land.

strait: A narrow body of water connecting two larger bodies of water.

vinaigrette: A tangy dressing made of oil, vinegar, and herbs that is used on salads, fish, and cold meats.

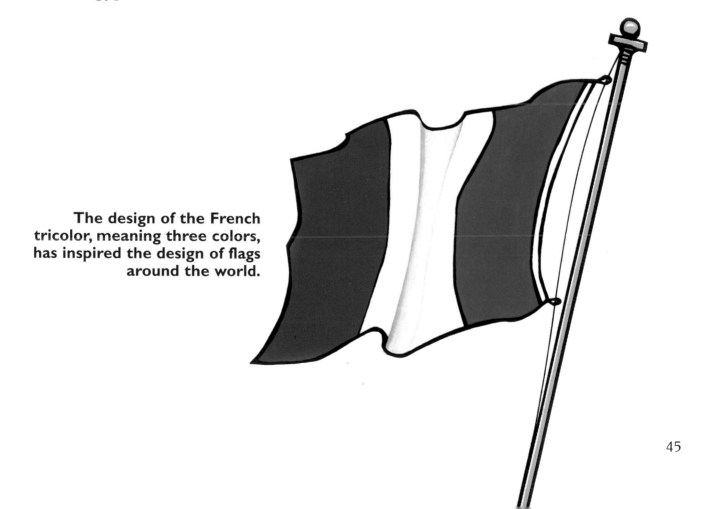

The design of the French tricolor, meaning three colors, has inspired the design of flags around the world.

Pronunciation Guide*

anglais	ah^n-GLAY
Arc de Triomphe	AHRK duh tree-OH^{n}F
bouillabaisse	boo-yuh-BEHS
Camembert	kah-mah^n-BEHR
centre aire	sah^n-TREHR
chien	SHYA^n
franglais	frah^n-GLAY
Gué	GAY
hypermarchés	ee-pehr-mahr-SHAY
Landes	LAH^{n}D
Lascaux	lah-SKOH
Loire	LWAHR
Louvre	LOO-vruh
Manche	MAH^{n}SH
marché aux puces	mahr-SHAY oh POOS
Marseillaise	mahr-say-YEHZ
Massif Central	mah-SEEF sah^n-TRAHL
Les Misérables	lay mee-zay-RAH-bluh
Pâques	PAHK
parlez-vous français	par-lay-VOO frah^n-SAY
pétanque	pay-TAH^{n}K
Poires Hélène	PWAHRZ ay-LEHN
Poisson d'avril	pwah-SOH^n dah-VREEL
Provence	proh-VAH^{n}S
République Française	ray-poo-BLEEK frah^n-SEHZ
Seine	SEHN
train à grande vitesse	TRA^n ah GRAH^{n}D vee-TEHS
Versailles	vehr-SY

*Translations are approximate.

Further Reading

Axworthy, Anni. *Anni's Diary of France*. Dallas: Whispering Coyote Press, 1994.

Carter, Angela. *Sleeping Beauty and Other Favourite Fairy Tales*. London: Victor Gollancz, 1982.

Chenevière, Alain. *Maud in France*. Minneapolis: Lerner Publications Company, 1996.

Chrisp, Peter. *The Normans*. New York: Thomson Learning, 1995.

France in Pictures. Minneapolis: Lerner Publications Company, 1991.

Garland, Michael. *Dinner at Magritte's*. New York: Dutton Children's Books, 1995.

Kristy, Davida. *Coubertin's Olympics: How the Games Began*. Minneapolis: Lerner Publications Company, 1995.

Moore, Robin. *The Hunchback of Notre Dame*, retold from Victor Hugo. New York: Simon and Schuster Children's, 1995.

Picard, Barbara L. *French Legends, Tales and Fairy Stories*. New York: Henry Z. Walck, 1955.

Porter, A. P. *Greg LeMond, Premier Cyclist*. Minneapolis: Lerner Publications Company, 1990.

Saint-Exupéry, Antoine de. *The Little Prince*. San Diego: Harcourt Brace and Co., 1971.

Waldee, Lynn Marie. *Cooking the French Way*. Minneapolis: Lerner Publications Company, 1982.

Wright, Nicola. *Getting to Know France and French*. Hauppauge, NY: Barron's Educational Series, 1993.

Metric Conversion Chart

WHEN YOU KNOW:	MULTIPLY BY:	TO FIND:
teaspoon	5.0	milliliters
Tablespoon	15.0	milliliters
cup	0.24	liters
inches	2.54	centimeters
feet	0.3048	meters
miles	1.609	kilometers
square miles	2.59	square kilometers
degrees Fahrenheit	5/9 (after subtracting 32)	degrees Celsius

Index